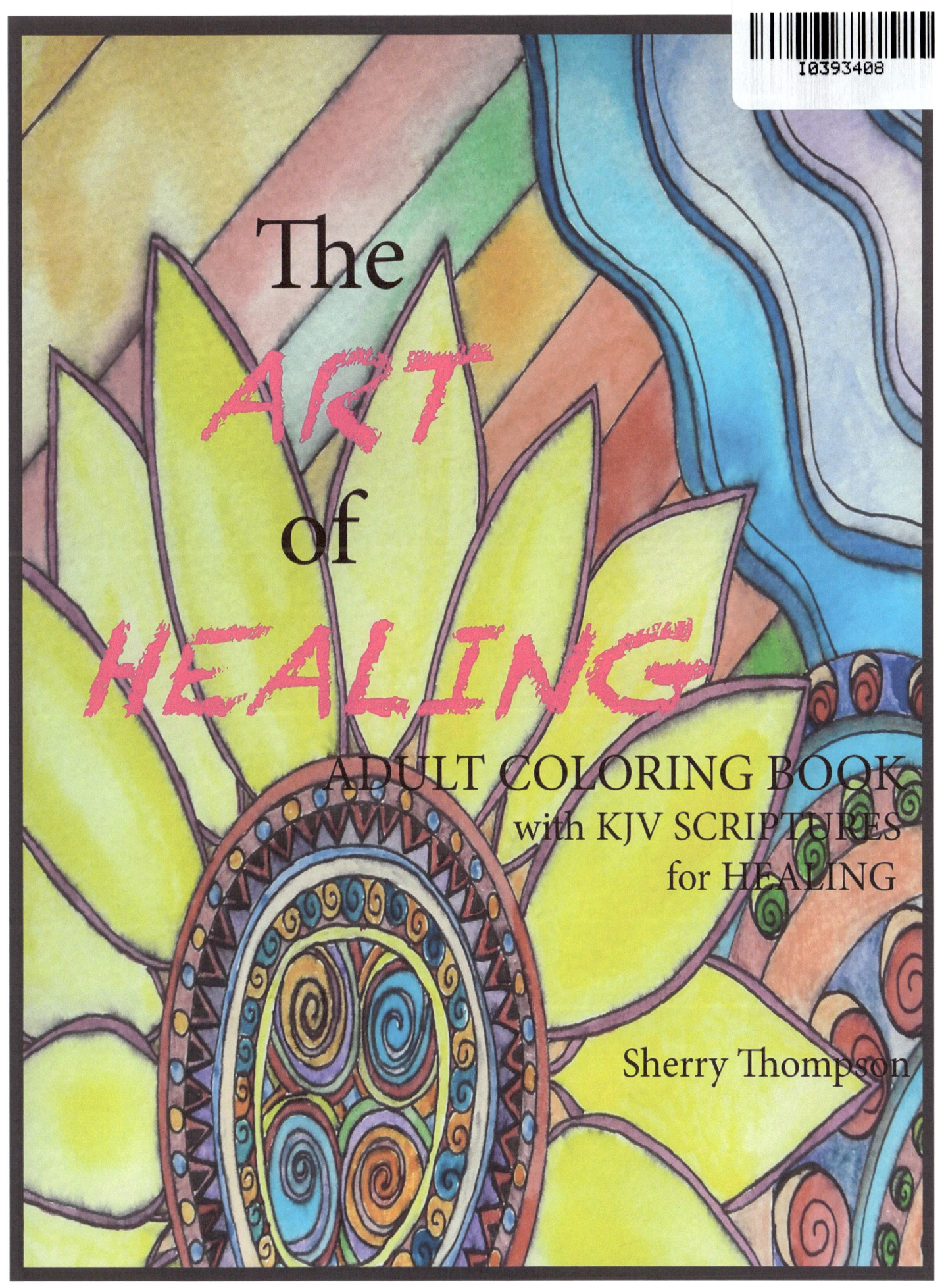

The ART of HEALING

ADULT COLORING BOOK
with KJV SCRIPTURES
for HEALING

Sherry Thompson

"Are they not all ministering spirits, sent forth to minister for them who shall be heirs of **salvation**?"

HEBREWS 1:14
KJV

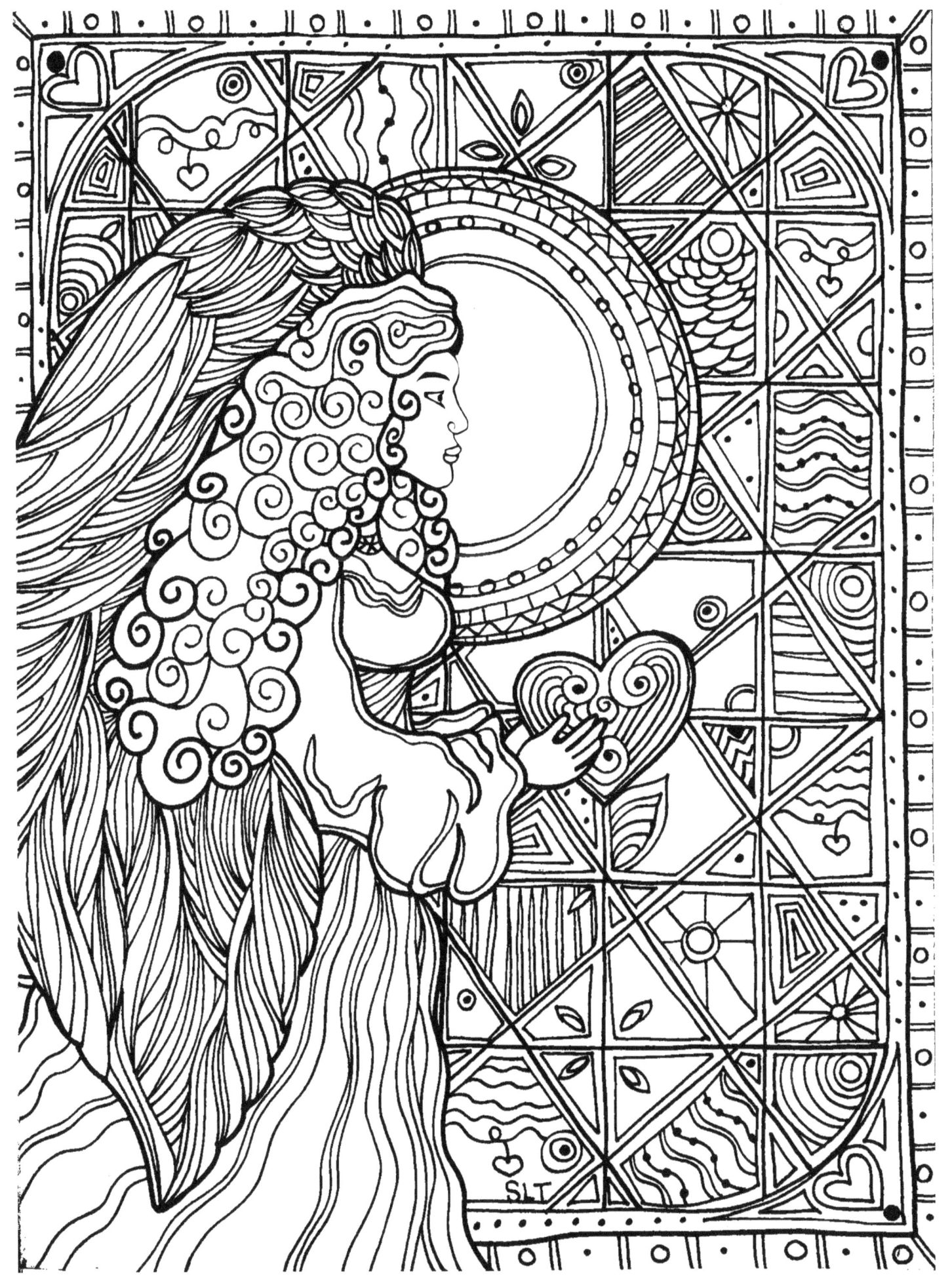

GENESIS 1: 30

"And to every beast of the earth, and to every fowl of the air, and to every thing that creepeth upon the earth, wherein there is **life**, I have given every green herb for meat: and it was so."

KJV

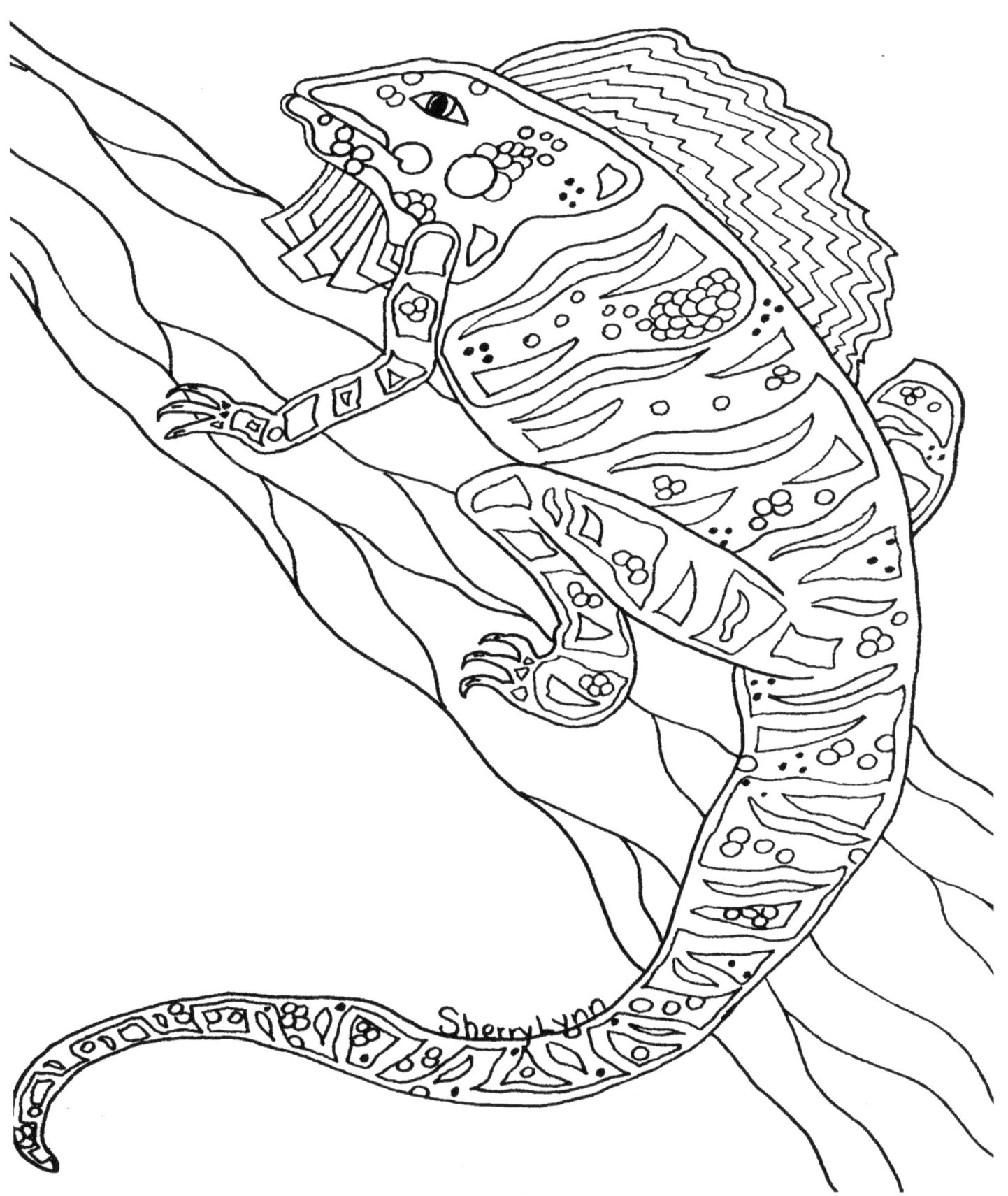

JAMES 3: 7

"For every kind of beasts,
and of birds, and of serpents,
and of things in the sea,
is tamed, and hath been
tamed of **mankind**."

KJV

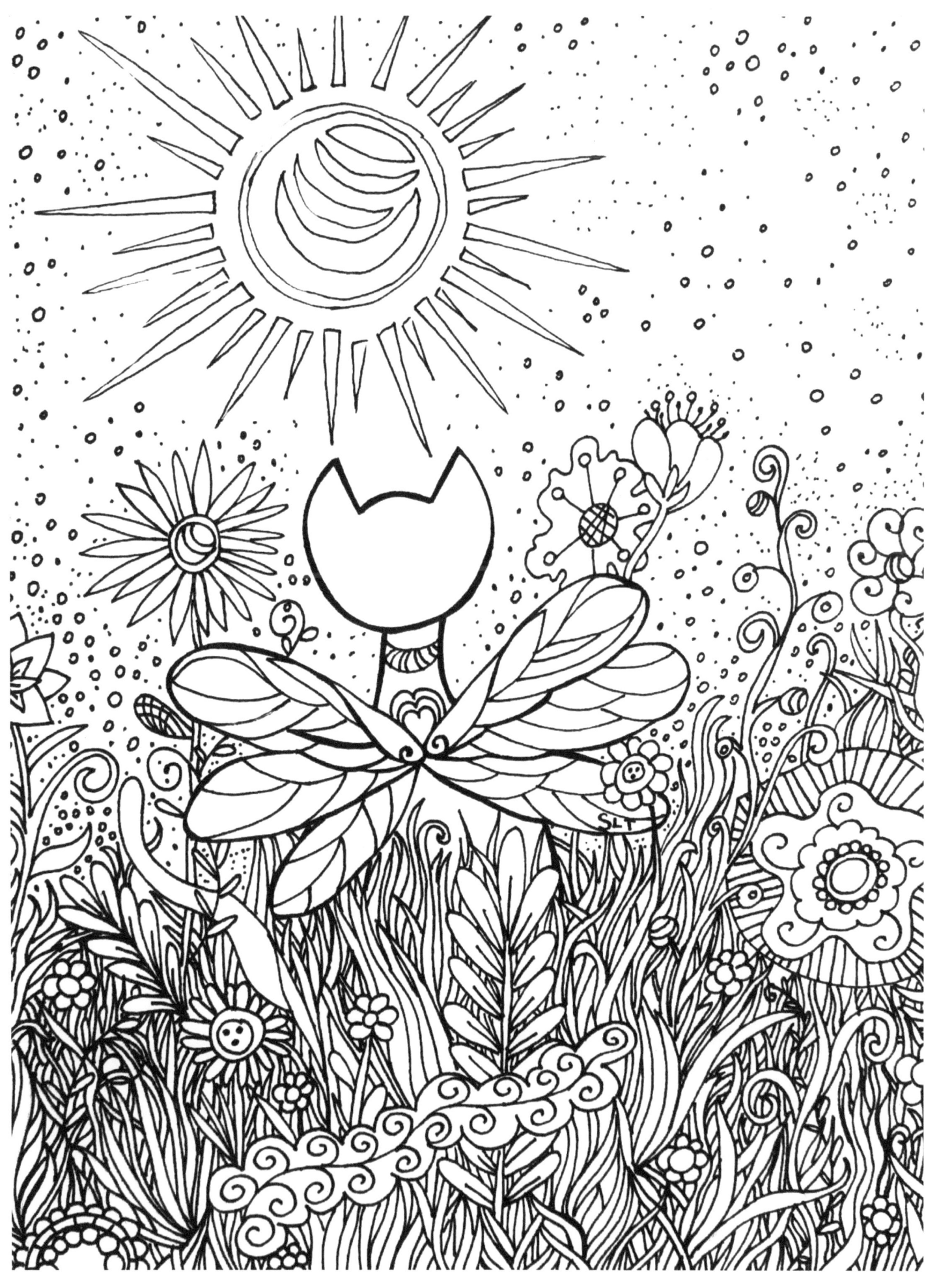

GENESIS 1:21

"And **GOD** created great whales, and every living creature that moveth, which the waters brought forth abundantly, after their kind, and every winged fowl after after his kind: and GOD saw that it was good."

KJV

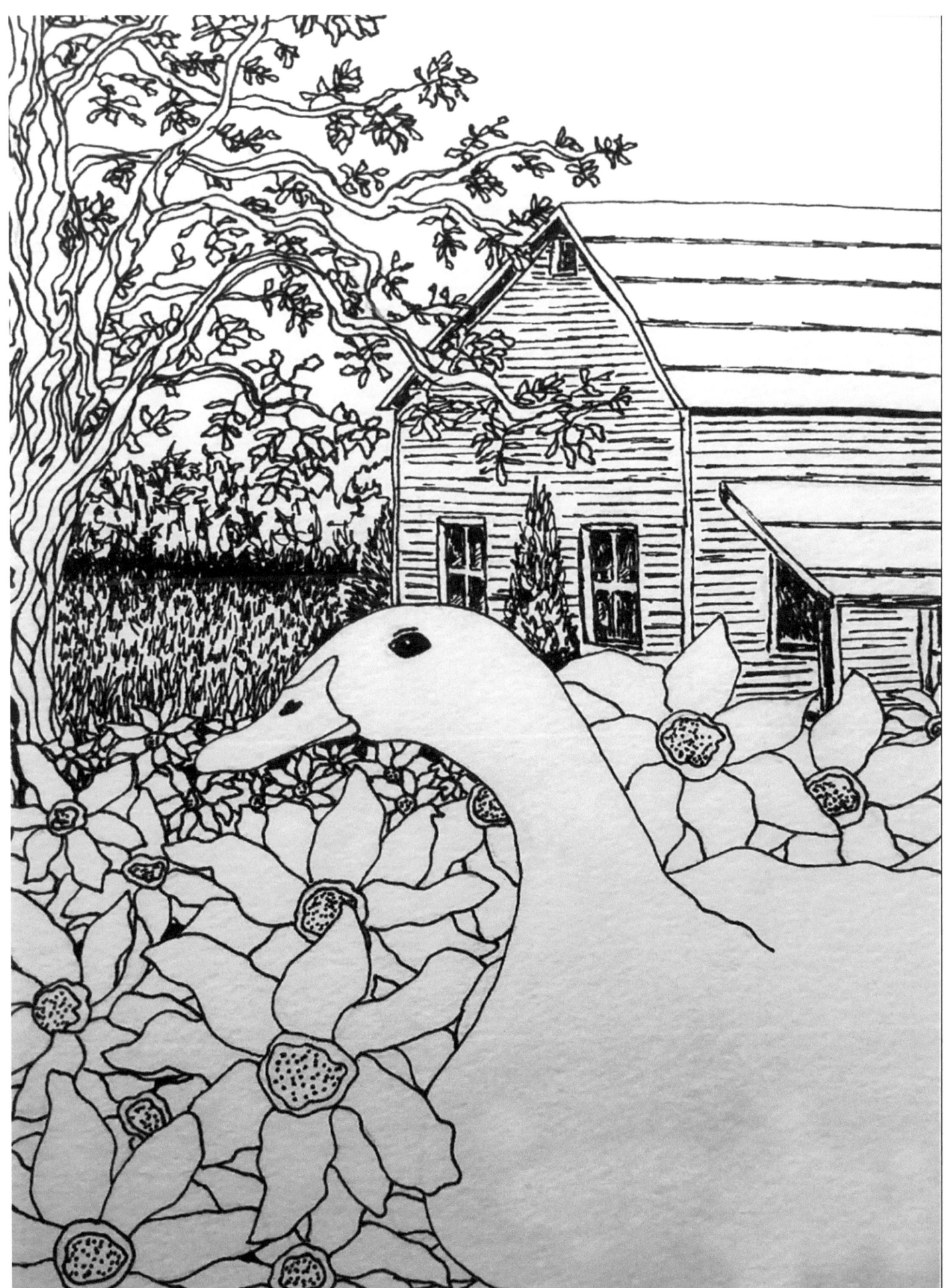

PSALMS 50:11

"I know all the fowls of the
mountains: and the wild
beasts of the field are **Mine**."

KJV

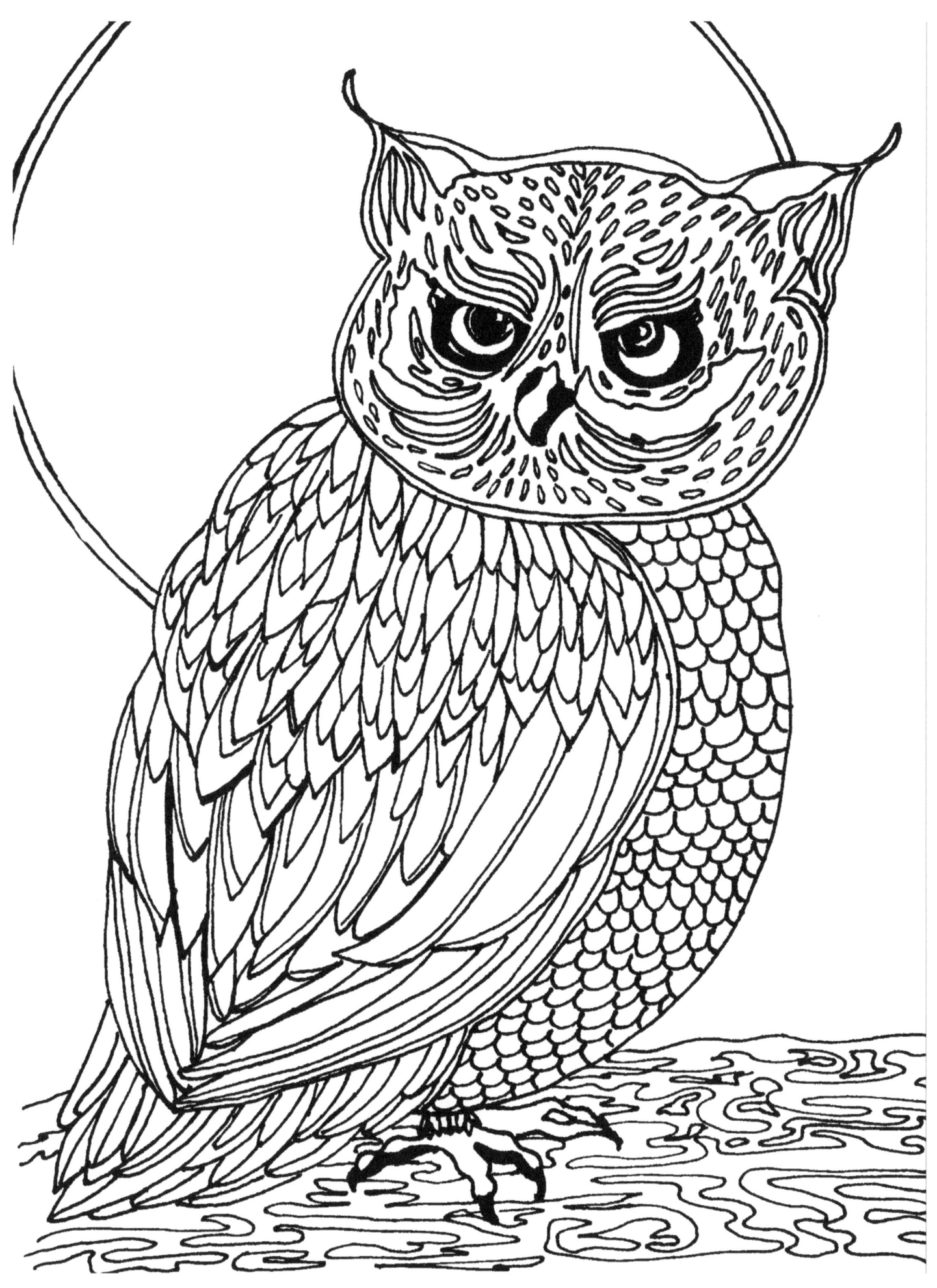

ISAIAH 40: 8

"The grass withereth, the flower fadeth: but the **word** of our GOD shall stand for ever."

KJV

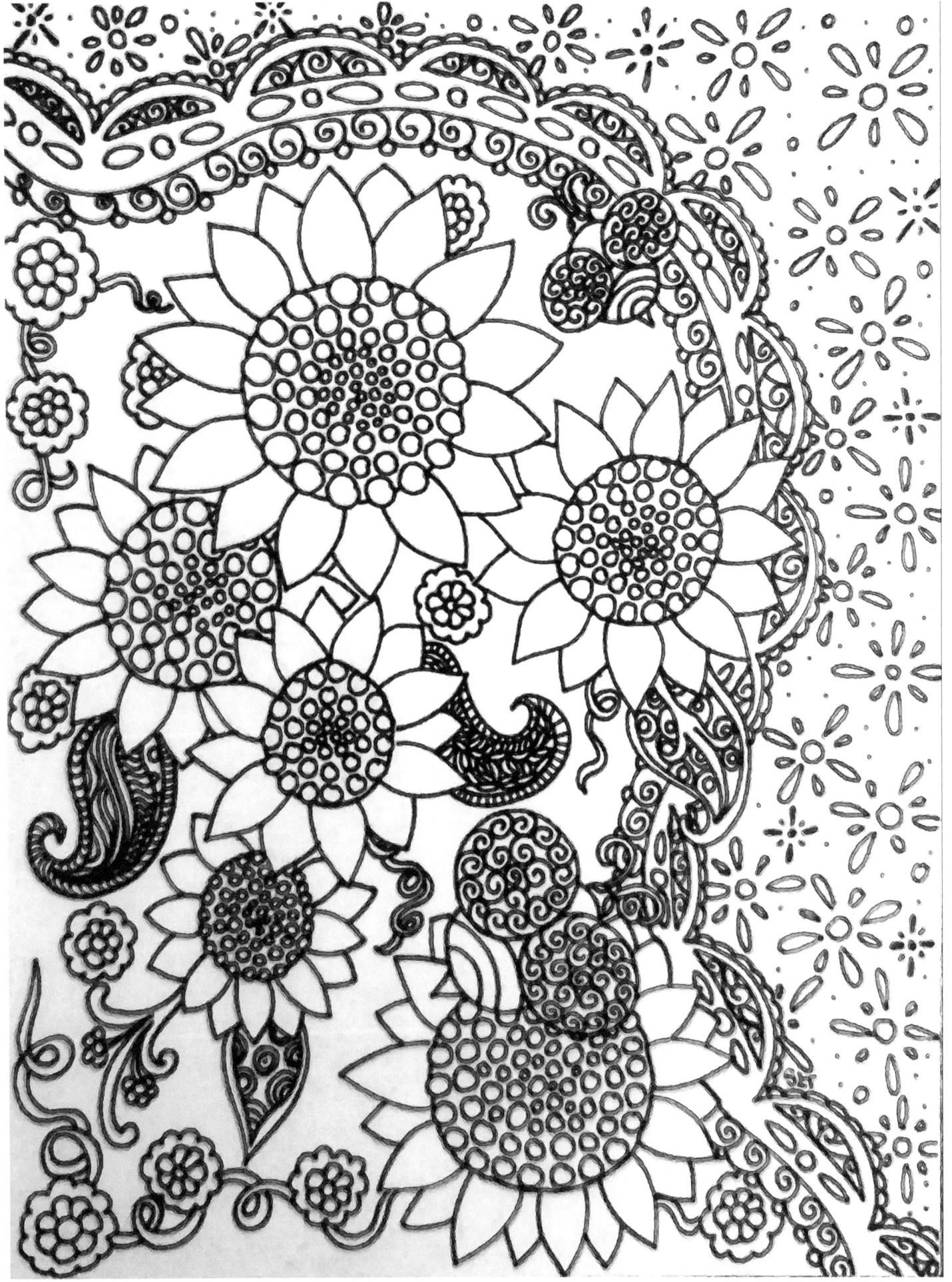

PSALMS 104: 24

"O LORD, how manifold are Thy works! In **wisdom** hast thou made them all: the earth is full of thy riches."

KJV

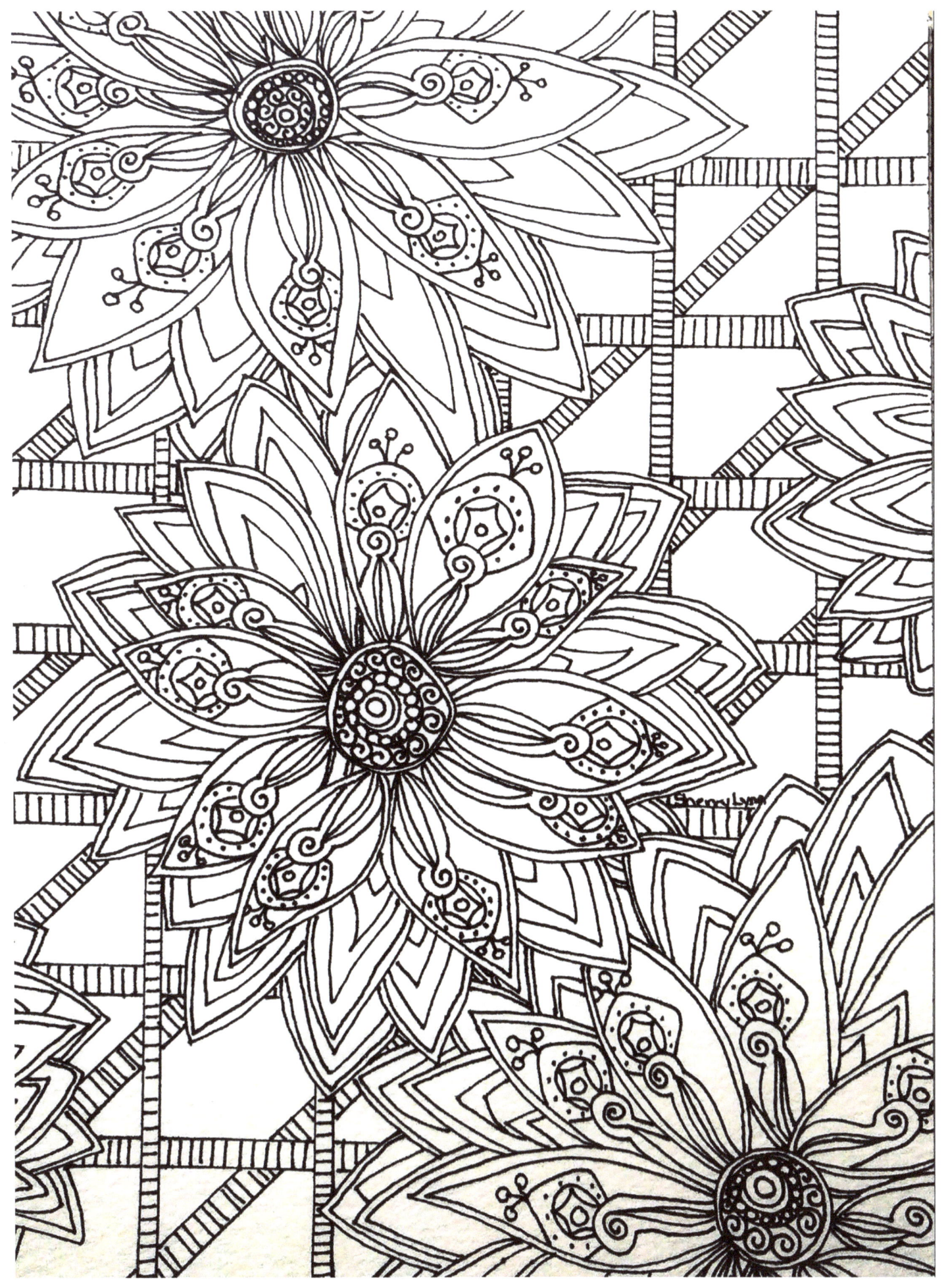

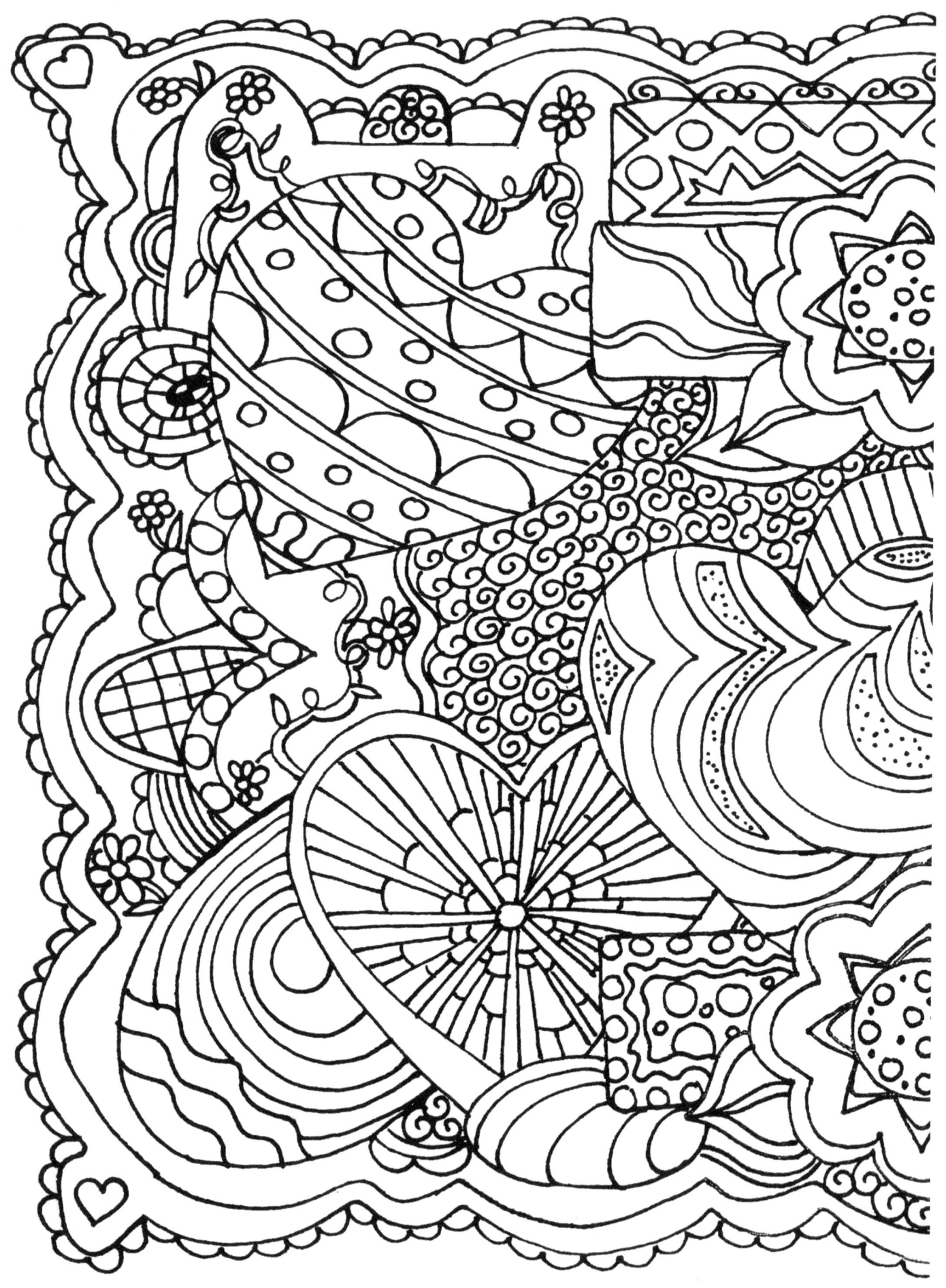

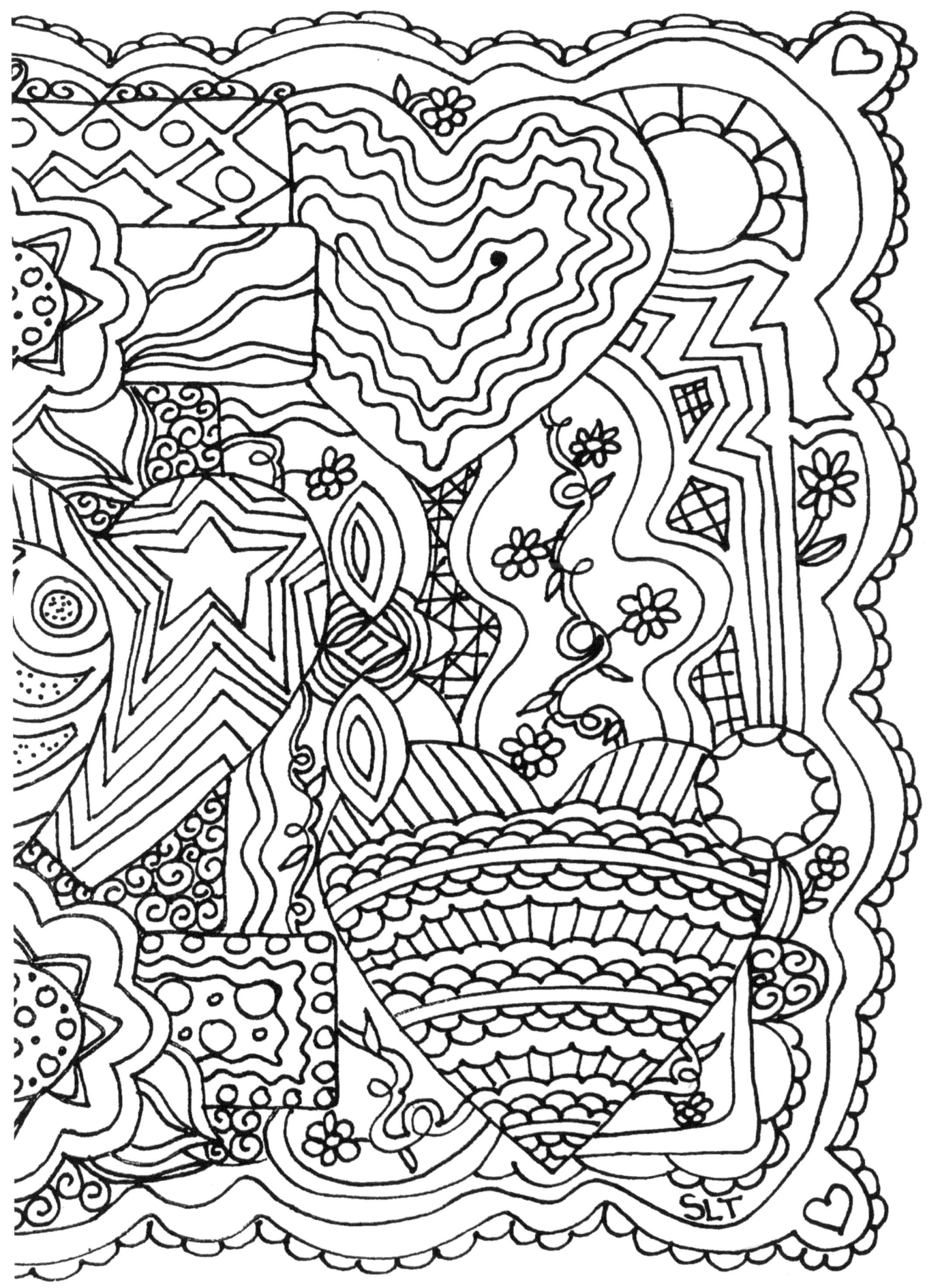

"For
He shall give
His **Angels**
charge over thee,
to keep thee in
all thy ways."

PSALMS 91:11

KJV

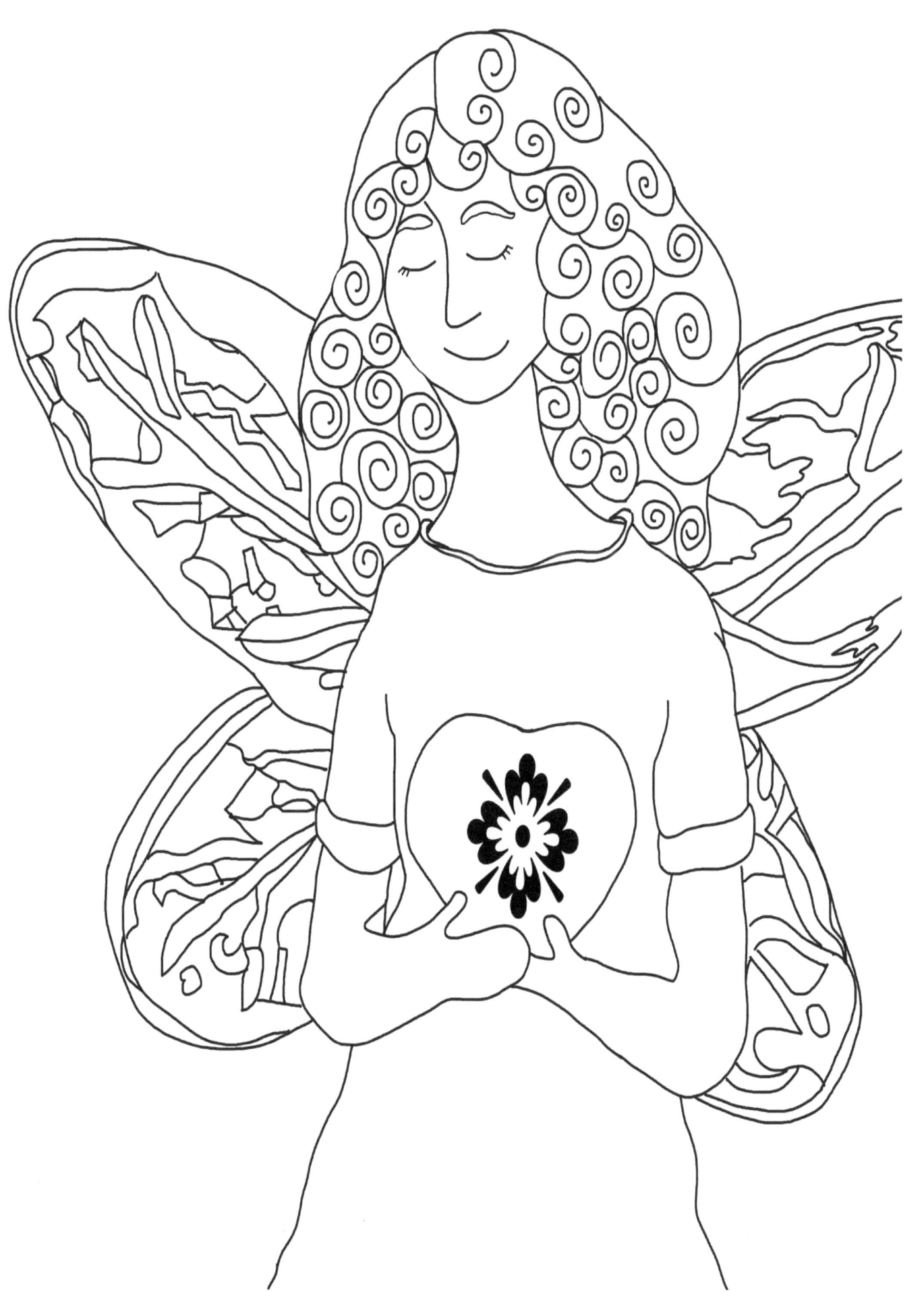

15 As for man, his **days** are
as grass: as a flower
of the field, so he flourisheth.

16 For the wind passeth
over it, and it is gone;
and the place thereof
shall know it no more.

KJV

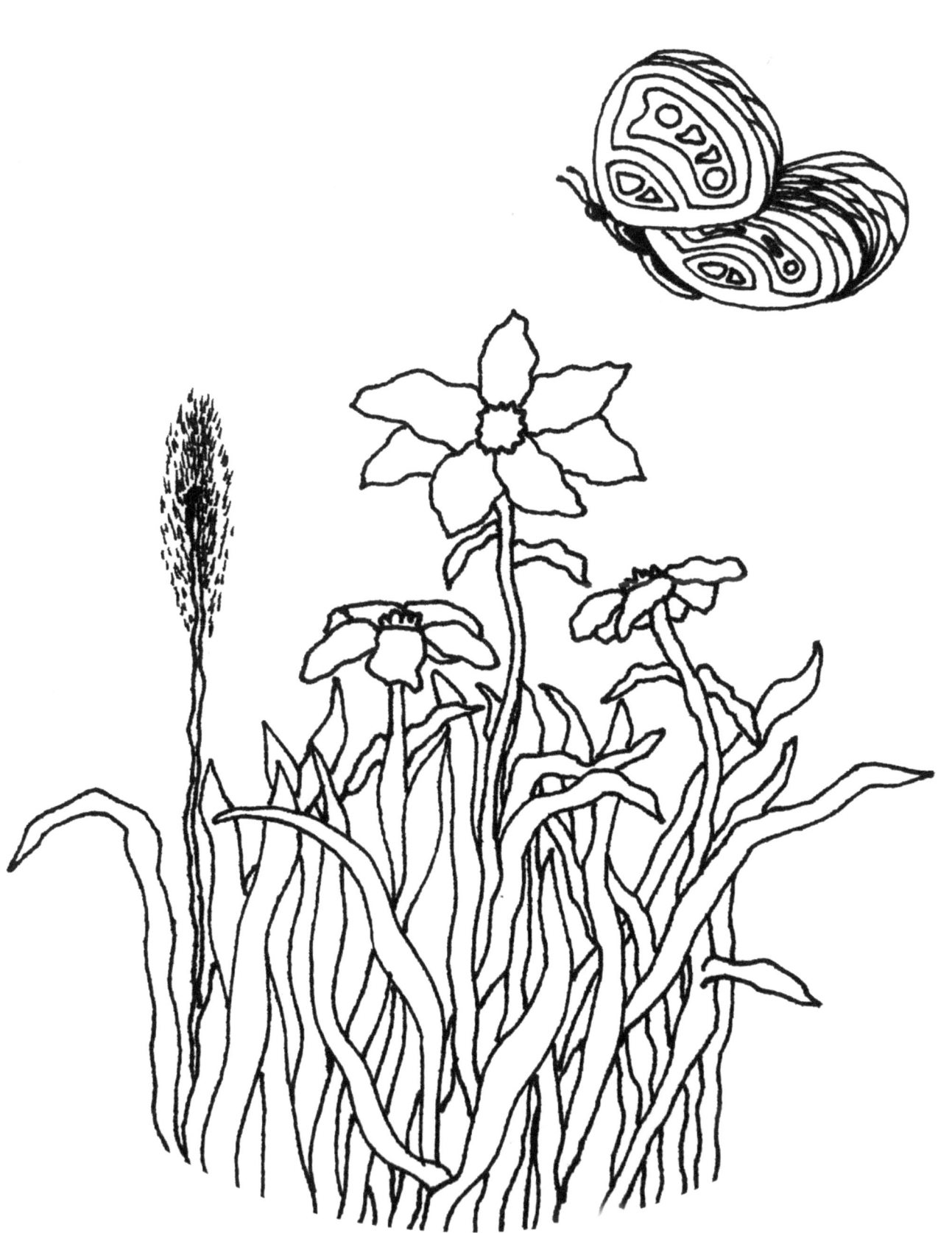

PSALMS 91: 1

"He that dwelleth in the secret place of the most High shall abide under the shadow of the **Almightly**."

KJV

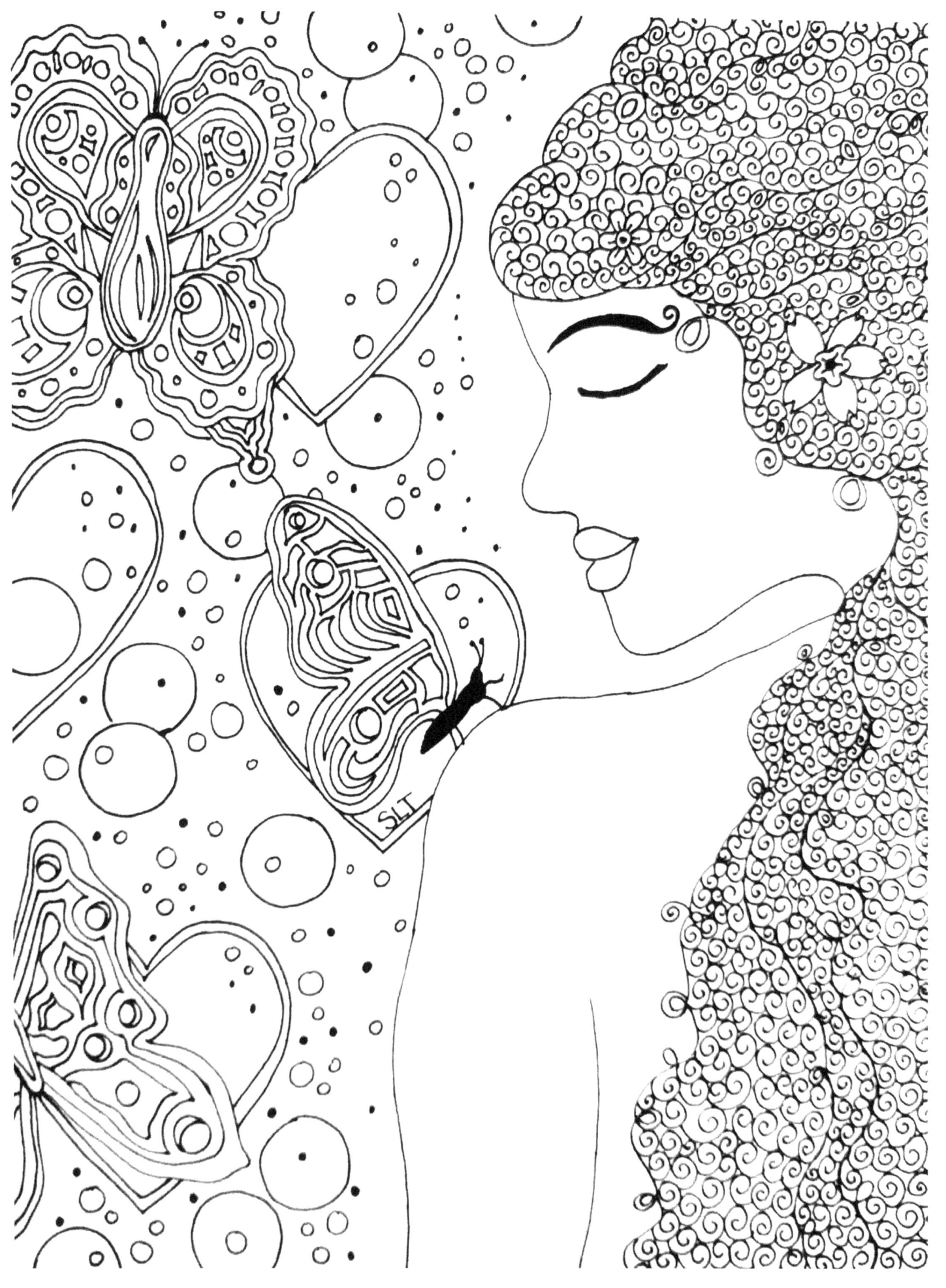

A new commandment I
give unto you,
that ye **love**
one another;
as I have loved you,
that ye also love
one another.

JOHN 13: 34-35
KJV

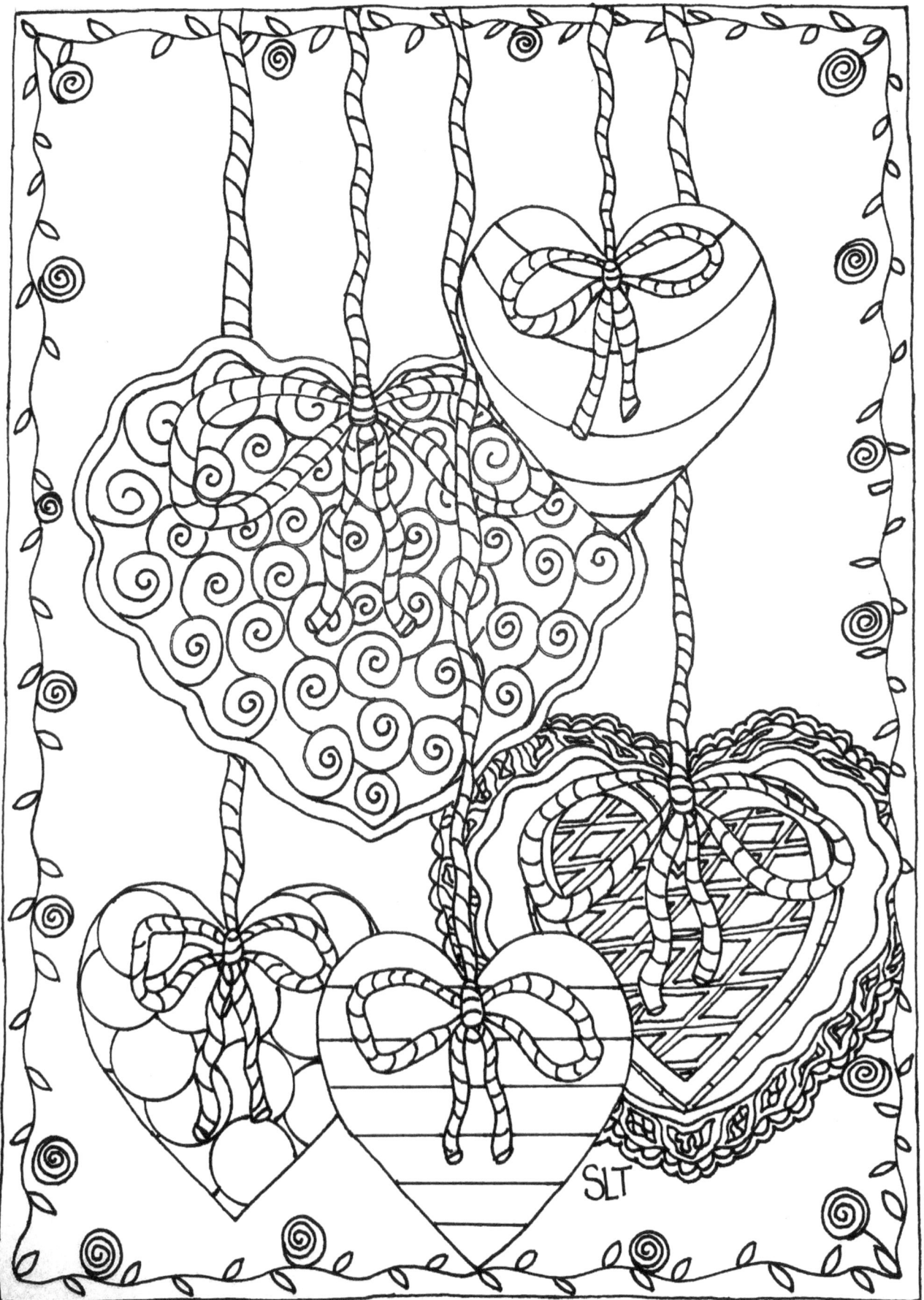

PSALMS 91: 2

"I will say of the LORD,
He is my **refuge** and my
fortress: my GOD;
in Him will I trust."

KJV

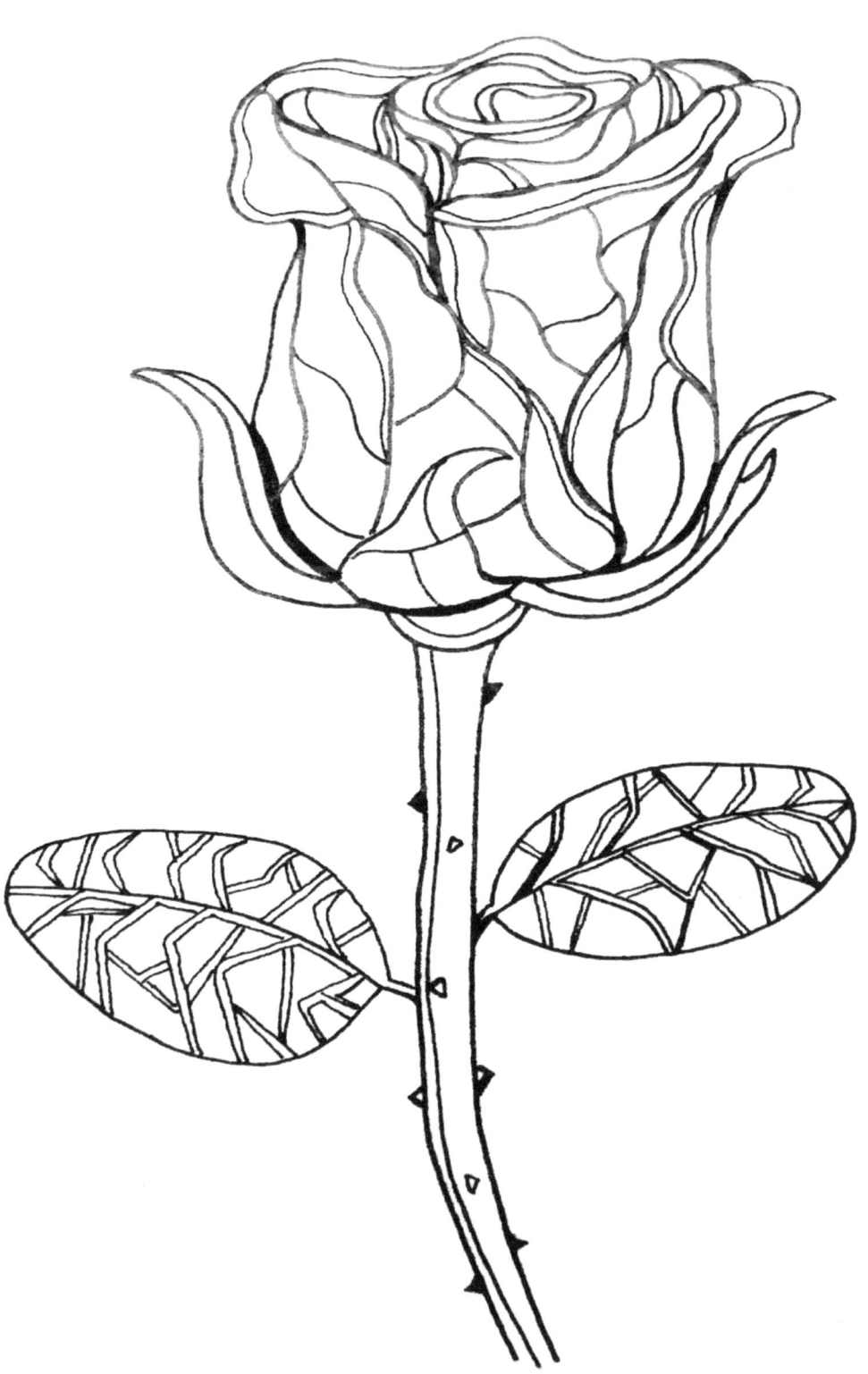

ISAIAH 65:25

"The wolf and the lamb shall feed together, and the lion shall eat straw like the bullock: and dust shall be the serpent's meat. They shall not hurt nor destroy in all my holy mountain, Saith the **LORD**."

KJV

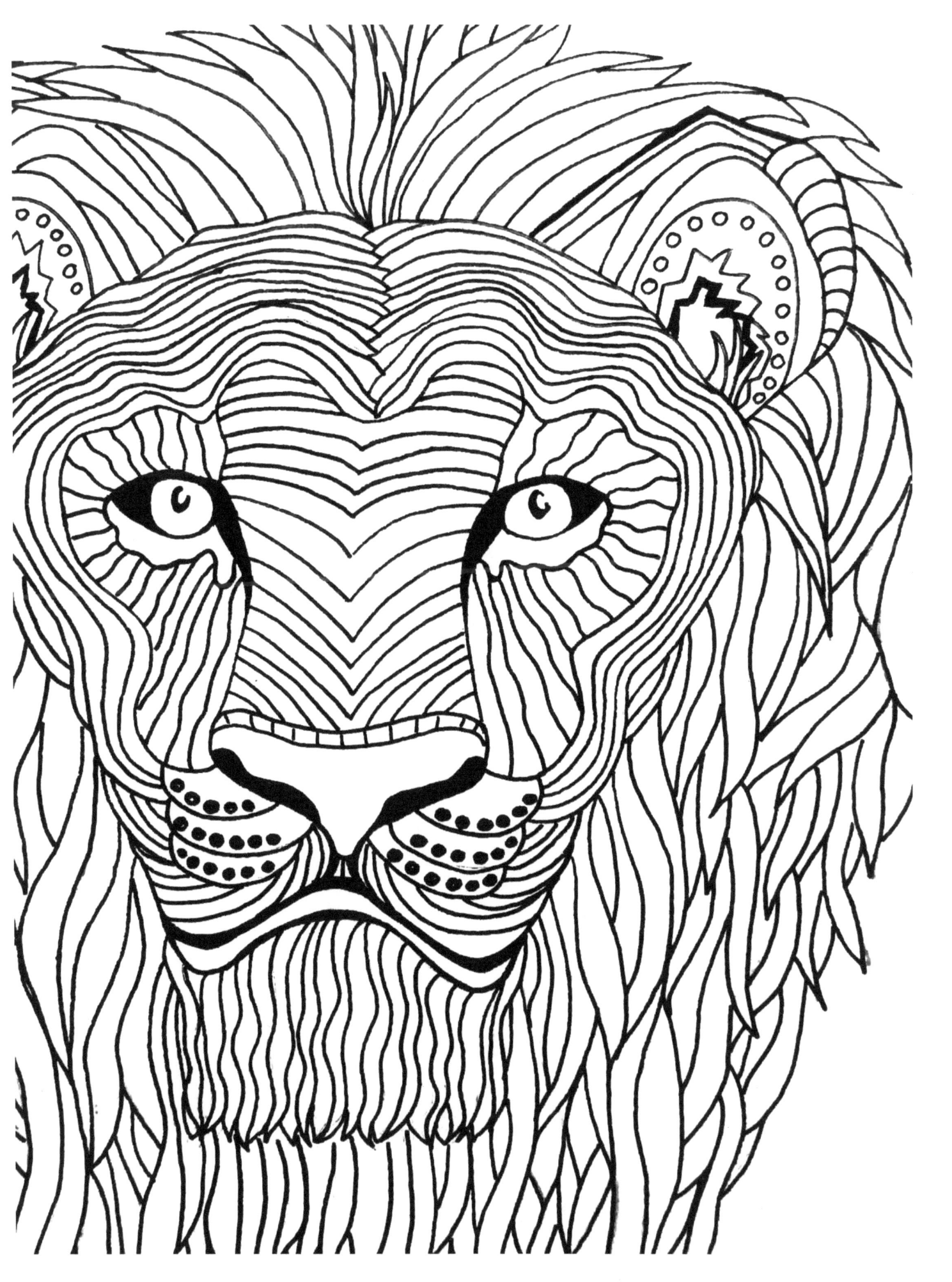

MATTHEW 6: 26
"Behold the fowls of the air:
for they sow not, neither do
they reap, nor gather into
barns; yet your heavenly
Father feedeth them.
Are ye not much
better than they?"
KJV

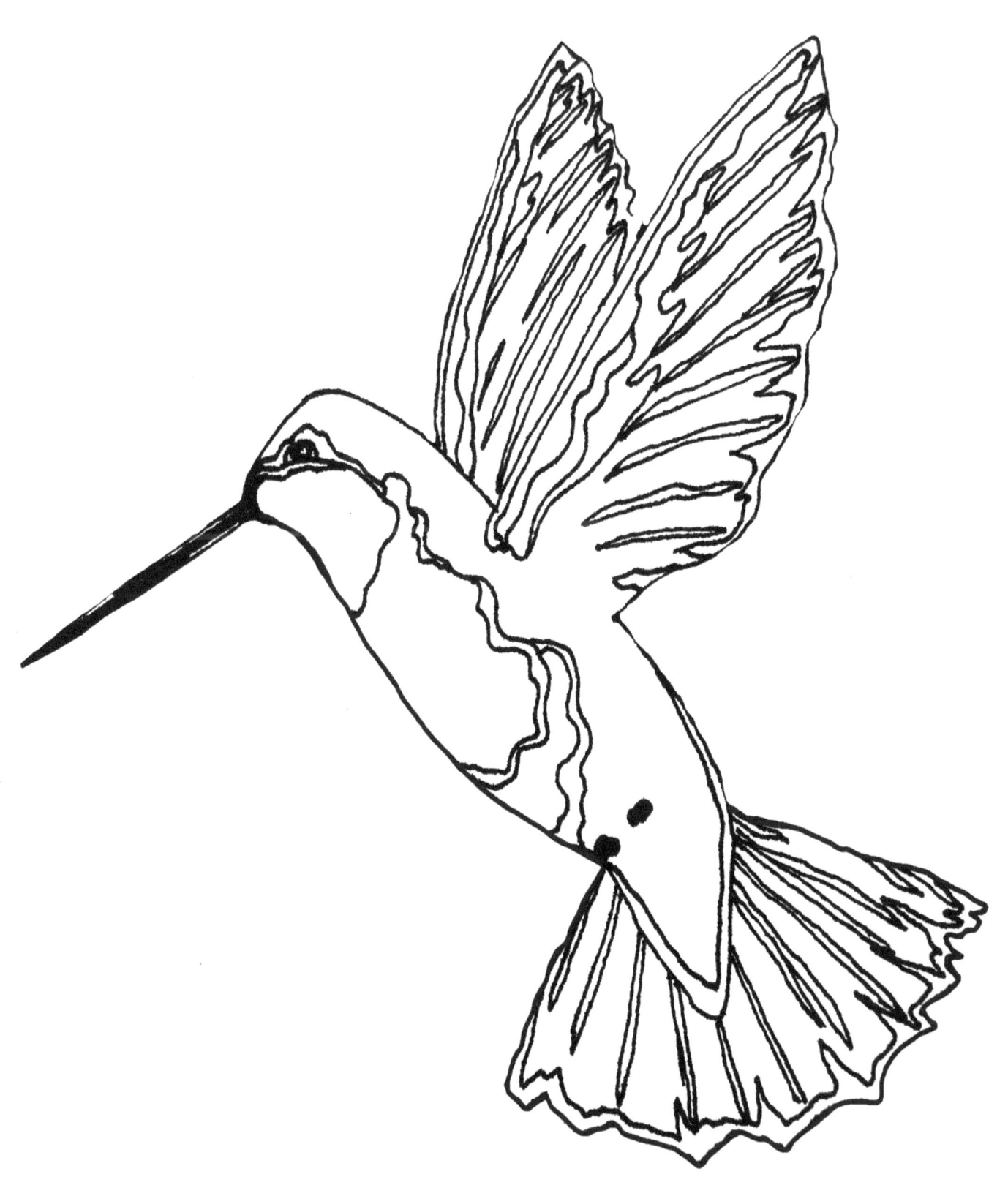

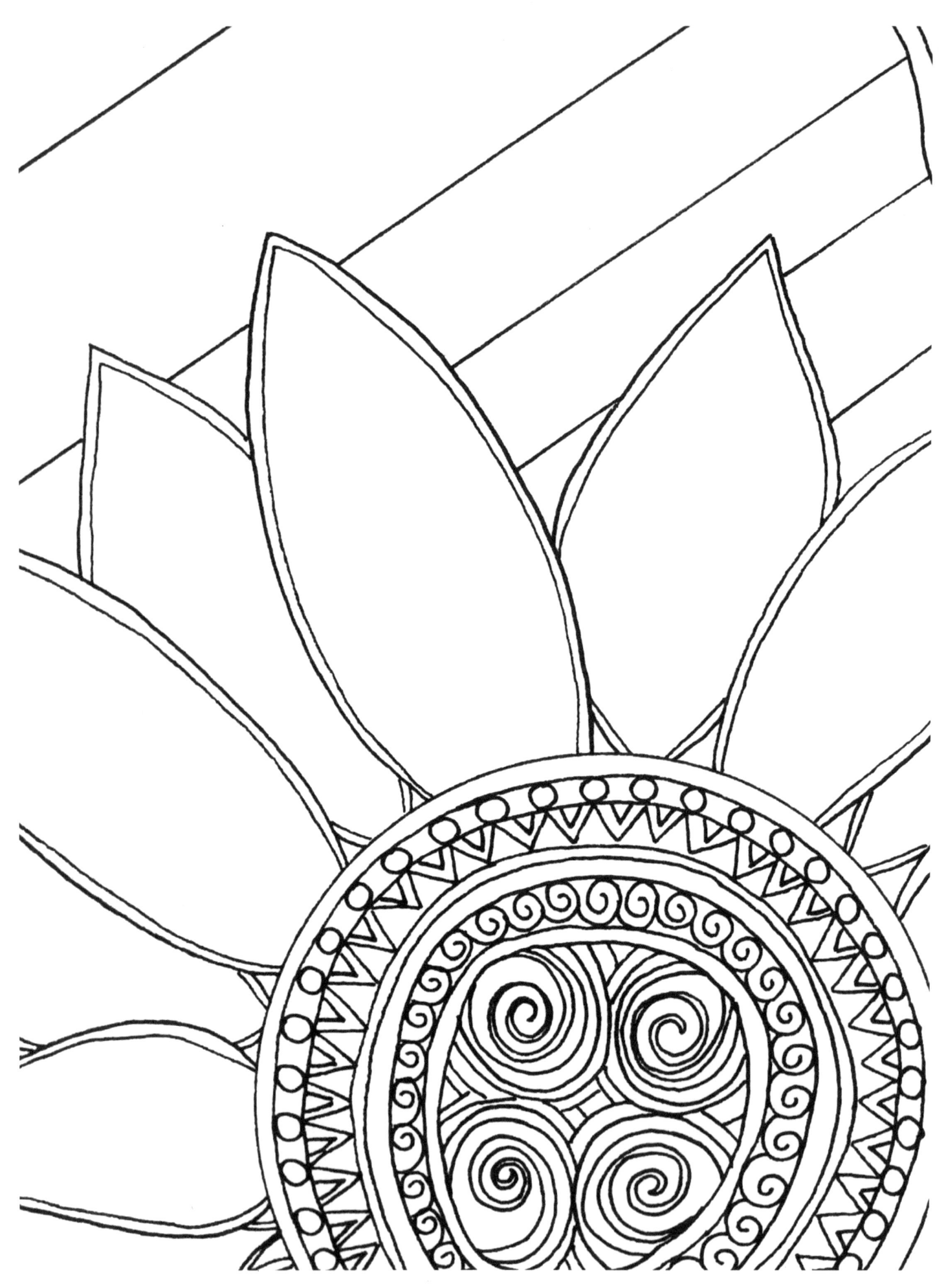

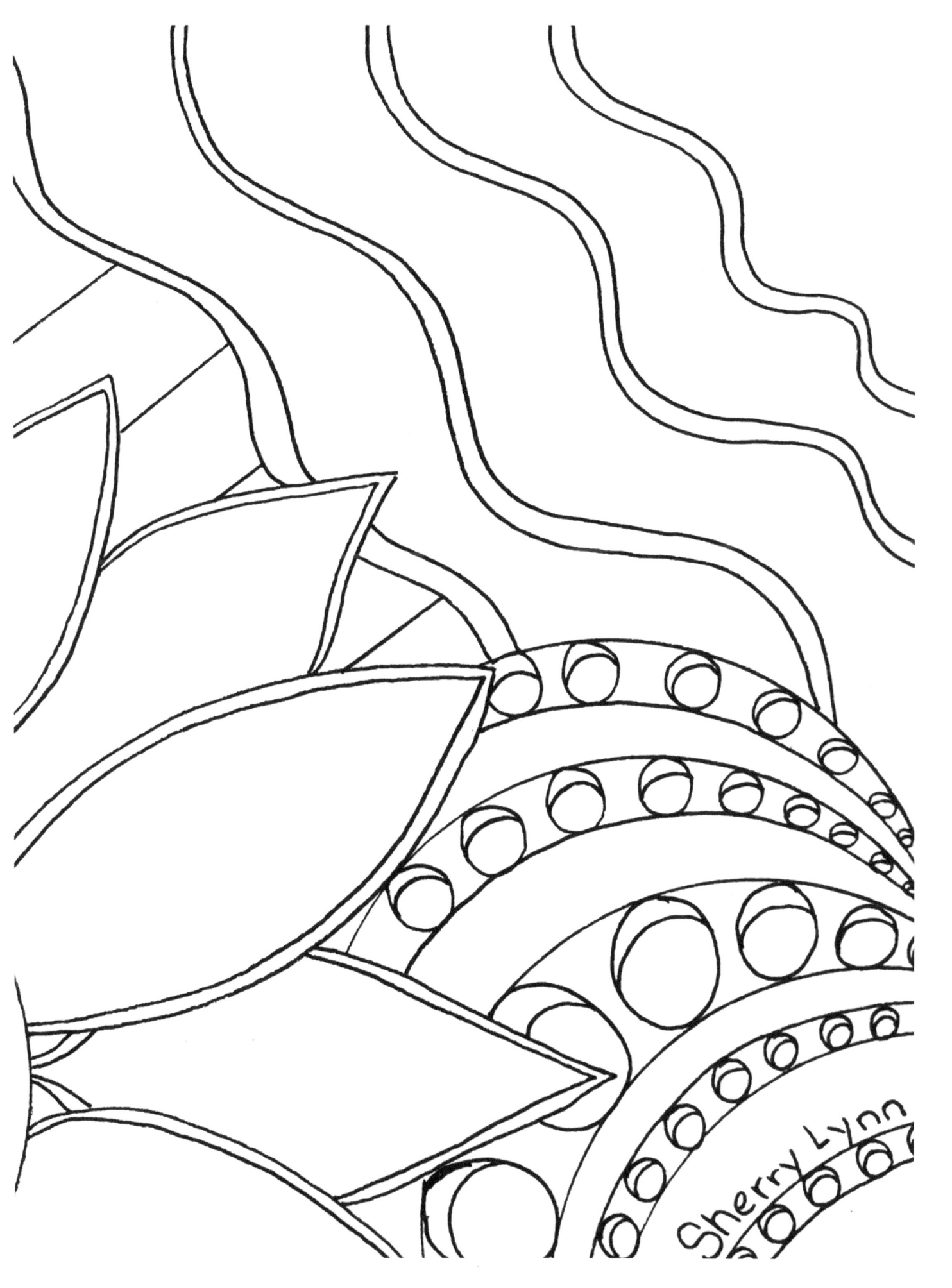

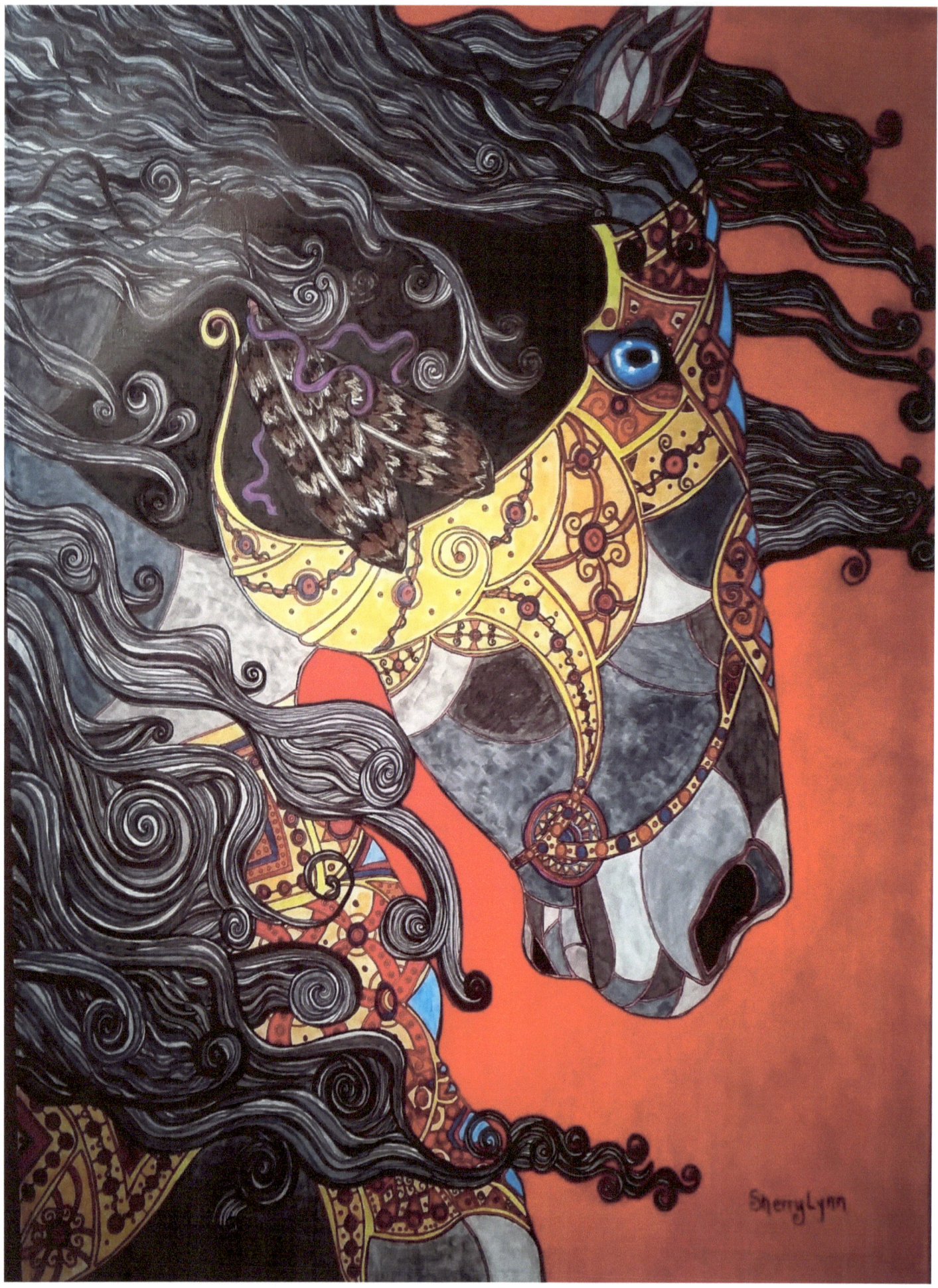

Sherry Lynn

www.ingramcontent.com/pod-product-compliance
Lightning Source LLC
Chambersburg PA
CBHW041318180526
45172CB00004B/1149